BRITISH MUSEUM PAPER PAGEANTS
GREEKS

Designed and illustrated by
BEVERLY SAUNDERS

JONATHAN CAPE
in association with
BRITISH MUSEUM PUBLICATIONS

INTRODUCTION

Greece is a dry and mountainous country, surrounded by many beautiful islands. Its people are never far from the sea, which has always played an important role in their lives, both for trade and transport.

The history of the Greeks spans thousands of years. Archaeologists have traced their origins to the primitive hunters of the *Stone Age*. Many different and fascinating civilisations have come and gone, including the *Minoan* Kings on the island of Crete with their beautiful palaces, and the powerful Mycenean rulers on the mainland.

Following these enlightened civilisations came the *Dark Ages*, a bitter time of wars and invasions. There followed a period in which great political changes took place. In many cities small groups of noblemen, known as *oligarchies*, overthrew the ruling Kings and established their own, often unjust, systems of law and order. Many people disliked their rule, so helped to put individual tyrants into power instead. If the tyrant was fair this was successful, but all too often he was cruel and unjust.

By the *Classical* period some tyrants had been replaced by *democracies*. Athens, for example, was one of many *city states*. Its government was fairly elected by its citizens. Not everyone could be a citizen, however: women, foreigners, slaves and freed slaves were all excluded from citizenship.

The four scenes in this book offer a glimpse of what life might have been like for the citizens of a city state during the Classical period in ancient Greece. One scene is set in a temple courtyard during a religious festival, one shows a rowdy drinking party, the third features a busy harbour and the fourth a visit to the theatre.

SCENE 1: THE TEMPLE

Greek temples were the most important buildings in the cities. Many were built of marble and decorated with brightly painted sculptures.

Unlike religious buildings in other cultures, in which services are held before a congregation, the purpose of a Greek temple was to house an enormous statue of the god or goddess to whom it was dedicated. The altar was situated outside, so worship took place in the open air.

The Greeks believed in many different gods and told many stories about them. Every god or goddess looked after a different aspect of Greek life. For example, *Zeus*, the god of the sky and thunder, ruled all the gods on Mount Olympus. *Demeter*, his sister, was the goddess of the earth and corn. *Ares* was the god of war, and *Aphrodite* the goddess of love and beauty.

Each temple had a special treasury in which gifts were left for the gods by citizens wishing to win their favour. Daily religious rituals, such as offering food and burning incense, were performed by priests and priestesses.

In this scene a Greek temple is in the midst of a religious festival celebrating the local goddess. Work has stopped for the day and a number of festivities have been organised, including an athletics competition, a drama festival and a sacrificial feast in honour of the goddess of the temple.

As they proceed from the city to the temple, the local people are singing and dancing. At the front of the procession are the four *kanephoroi*, or basket bearers, dressed in colourful robes, carrying various offerings to the goddess and the sacred sacrificial knife on gold and silver dishes.

The priest prepares the altar and, after hymns and prayers, a young bullock is sacrificed and roasted over the altar fire. The meat is shared out among the people, who eat it with enjoyment. Meat is a rare luxury for the Greeks and many have looked forward to this treat for several weeks.

SCENE 2: A SYMPOSIUM

After a day spent in the *agora* (the commercial and political centre of the city), or maybe inspecting their farming estates in the countryside, wealthy Greek men often met at each other's homes to relax at a *symposium*.

This was an evening drinking party to which wives were not invited. Instead, beautiful female dancers and musicians were hired to entertain the guests. These *hetairai* were usually slave girls, especially trained in music schools to sing and dance. A symposium might have been like this scene.

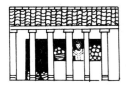

This evening the *andron* (dining-room) looks particularly impressive because important guests are expected. Flickering light from small oil lamps dances on the *mosaic* floor and casts shadows on the richly decorated walls. On one wall hang a *kithara* and a *lyre* (musical instruments). The other wall is decorated with a beautiful woollen textile, hand-woven by the host's wife.

Like most women from wealthy families, she spends much of her time in the women's quarters at the back of the house. She supervises the slaves in their daily household duties, and watches carefully as they dye and spin the wool for the lovely rugs, cushions and wall hangings which decorate the house. The mistress rarely leaves her home, perhaps only to attend religious festivals or to go on occasional shopping trips, when she has to be attended by a slave. To pass the time, she often invites her friends to her home, and as they work at their looms they talk about the latest gossip.

In the andron the master's guests have arrived. They have just enjoyed a delicious meal of fish, chicken and goat's cheese in honey, accompanied by leeks and beans in olive oil. The food has been cooked in small pottery ovens, or over the charcoal fire in the kitchen. The oil is from the host's own olive trees, and is such a useful and valuable commodity that the trees are protected by Greek law and cannot be cut down.

Two servant girls carry in dishes of fruits and nuts – oranges, grapes, pomegranates, figs and almonds. These are placed in front of the guests on small tables which can be slid out from under the couches when they are needed.

Wine is mixed with water in a large *krater* (mixing bowl), because it would be far too sweet and sickly otherwise. It is then served to the guests from small jugs, and the symposium proper begins.

First, a chubby comic amuses the guests with humorous stories, while jugglers and acrobats perform their tricks. Three beautiful musicians and a dancer all arrive and present each guest with a colourful wreath of flowers to wear. The musicians play the flute, kithara and lyre to accompany

the dancer as she weaves gracefully between the couches entertaining the guests. As the evening wears on, poetry and songs in praise of love are recited.

After several games of *kottabos*, in which wine dregs are flicked at a target, the tired but merry guests bid each other good night and make their way home by lamplight.

SCENE 3: THE HARBOUR

The sea was vital to almost every aspect of life in Greece, so her ports were important naval and commercial centres. This scene shows what a busy Greek harbour might have been like.

Money from rich silver mines has enabled Athens to build up the most powerful navy in Greece. A large *trireme*, or warship, has just returned from an important sea battle against the Persians, thus preventing a Persian

 invasion of the Greek mainland. On the upper deck stand several soldiers. All are Greek *citizens*, obliged by law to fight for their *city state* in the event of war. They are dressed in linen *cuirasses*, helmets and protective leg armour, and carry a decorated shield, a sword and a spear. All their armour has to be bought by the soldiers themselves, and those who cannot afford it become *rowers*, responsible for powering the enormous warship. Over one hundred oarsmen are crammed into the two lower decks. A small group of soldiers disembark, pleased to be home and on dry land again. Life on a crowded trireme is extremely uncomfortable, with little room for eating or sleeping.

Near by, a sturdy sailing ship is being loaded with Greek pottery. Together with wine, olive oil, silverware, statues and fine cloth, pottery is exported to the lands round the Mediterranean and Black Sea. Greek merchants all own their own ships, though many borrow money from bankers to finance their trading ventures.

In the background, grain is being unloaded on to the quayside. This is a vital import because poor farming land makes it difficult for Greece to produce enough to feed the population.

Later ships bearing timber, metals, perfumes, ivory and incense are expected to arrive from foreign countries. Local traders wander down to the harbour as another busy day of bargaining begins.

SCENE 4: THE THEATRE

Each spring the Athenians held a great religious festival to celebrate *Dionysus*, the god of wine. As part of the celebrations, choruses performed songs and dances often inspired by legends about Dionysus.

At the early festivals it is thought that the chorus chanted the stories in unison, but later one actor would separate from the rest to take the part of the story's main character. Eventually, his words and actions became more important than the songs and dances of the chorus. In time the number of actors was increased to three; they were all men, even for the female roles. This was the beginning of the modern play as we know it.

There were two main types of Greek play – *tragedies* and *comedies*. Tragedies re-enacted stories based on myths already familiar to the audience.

The actors wore long, colourful robes and special boots called *korthoni*. Comedies were full of slapstick and vulgar jokes, often about well-known and respected Greek citizens. The actors' ridiculously padded costumes and silly antics kept the audience amused. Whatever the play, the actors and chorus wore stiff face masks with gaping mouths.

This scene shows what a Greek theatre might have looked like. The audience is sitting in the open air on banked tiers of stone seats. These are set into the sloping hillside and arranged around a circular paved area called the *orchestra*, where the chorus performs. In the centre stands an altar to the god, Dionysus. Behind the orchestra is the *skene* (stage building), painted to look like a Greek palace or temple.

Many of the audience arrived at sunrise to buy small bronze theatre tickets, which cost two *obols* each. If they cannot afford to pay, there is a special fund from which they can borrow the cost of a ticket. Coloured cushions are spread out on the hard seats, and food and drink unpacked. It will be a long day.

The opening tragedy is a bloody revenge, and the chorus recites the story of a terrible murder. Suddenly, an *ekkyklema* (small platform) is wheeled through the central door of the skene and the murderess and her victim are revealed. The horrible crime has to be presented in this way because violent scenes are never acted out on the stage in Greek drama.

There are several more plays, and then at the end of the day the judges, who sit on the front row with the priests of Dionysus, present an ivy wreath to the best playwright.

Cut along

Fold back and glue to temple-scene floor

Fold back and glue to symposium - scene floor

Cut along ⊳⊸

Temple - Strip A

Temple - Strip B

Fold back and glue to theatre – scene floor

Cut along

Fold back and glue to harbour - scene floor

Cut along

Cut out ✂

Cut out ✂

Fold forwards

Fold backwards

Cut out ✂

Cut out ✂

Cut out ✂

Fold forwards | Fold backwards

Fold backwards

Fold forwards

Cut out.

Stand the Chorus in the theatre

Cut out ✂

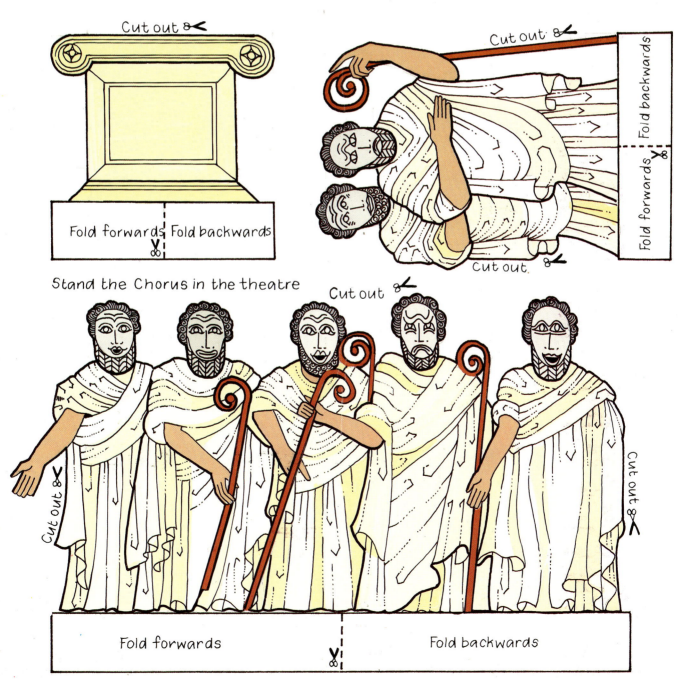

Cut out ✂

Cut out ✂

Fold forwards

Fold backwards

Cut out ✂

Cut out ✂

Fold forwards

Fold backwards

Cut out ✂

Cut out ✂

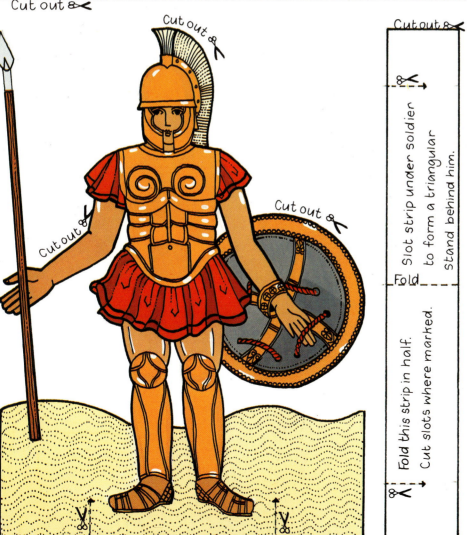

Cut out ✂

Cut out ✂

Cut out ✂

Cut out ✂

Cut out ✂

Fold this strip in half.
Cut slots where marked.

Fold

Slot strip under soldier
to form a triangular
stand behind him.

Cut out ✂

These soldiers have just disembarked from the trireme.
Stand them in the harbour.

Three musicians and a dancing girl. Stand them in the andron.

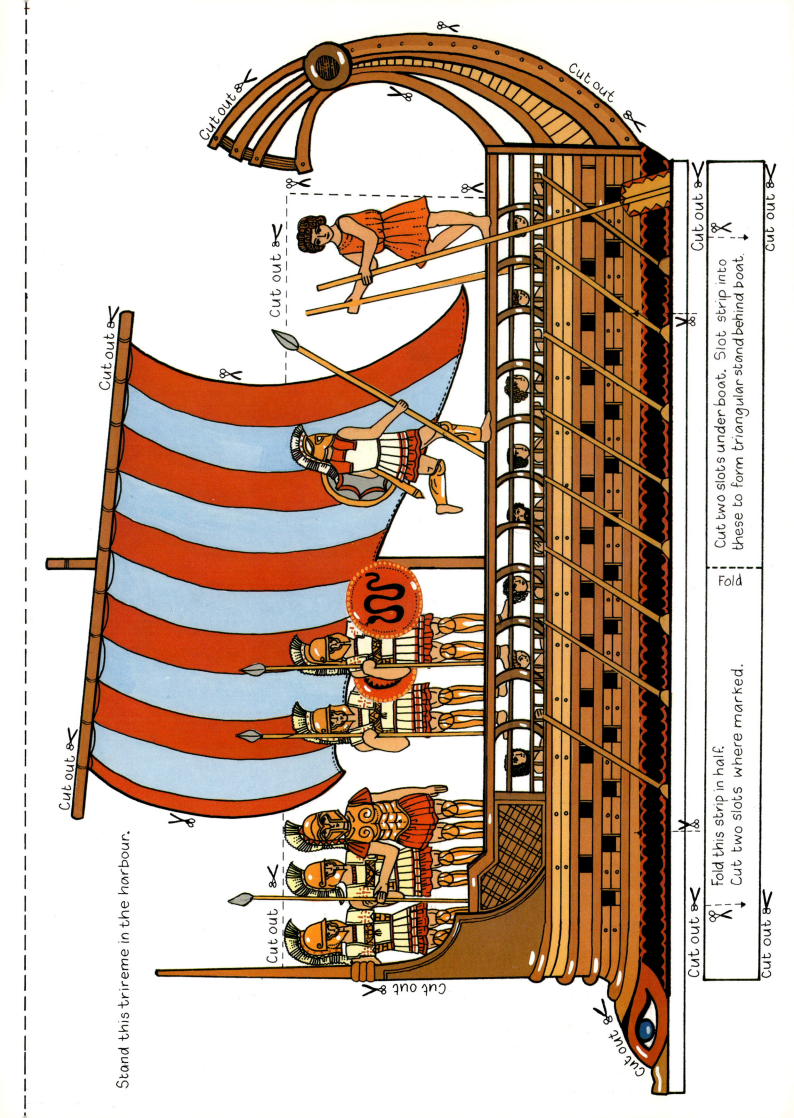

Stand this trireme in the harbour.

Cut out

Cut out

Cut out

Cut out

Cut out

Cut out

Cut out

Cut out

Cut out

Cut out

Cut out

Cut out

Cut out

Cut out

Cut out

Cut two slots under boat. Slot strip into these to form triangular stand behind boat.

Fold

Fold this strip in half. Cut two slots where marked.

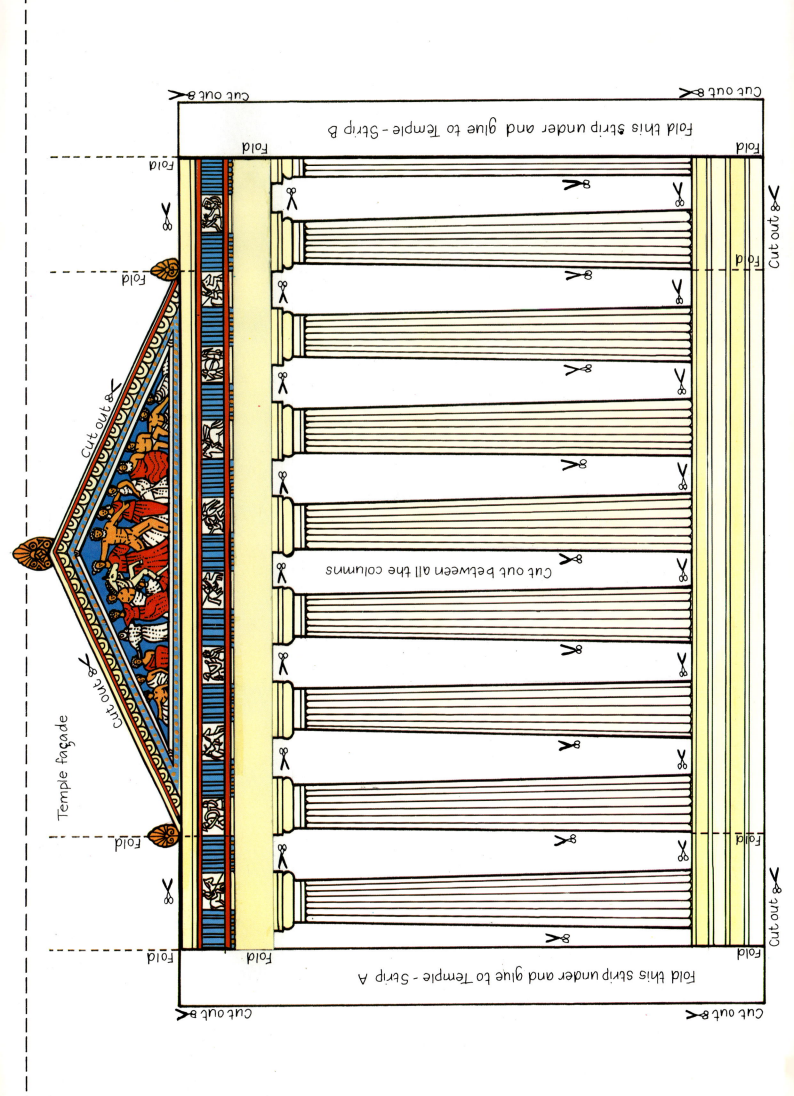

Temple façade

Fold this strip under and glue to Temple - Strip B

Fold this strip under and glue to Temple - Strip A

Cut out between all the columns

Cut out

Cut out

Cut out

Cut out

Fold

Fold

Fold

Fold

Cut out ✂

Cut out ✂

Cut out ✂

Cut out ✂

Fold forwards | Fold backwards

The priest leads a procession to the sacrificial altar.

Cut out ✂

Cut out ✂

Cut out ✂

Cut out ✂

Fold forwards | Fold backwards

Stand the sacrificial fire in front of the temple. Arrange the figures around it.

Cut out ✂

Cut out ✂

Cut out ✂

Cut out ✂

Fold forwards | Fold backwards

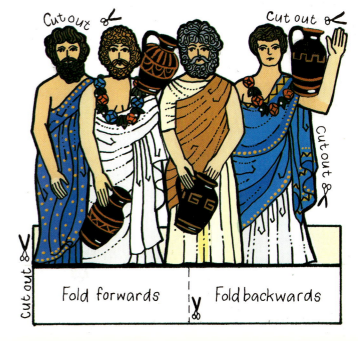

Cut out ✂

Cut out ✂

Cut out ✂

Cut out ✂

Fold forwards | Fold backwards

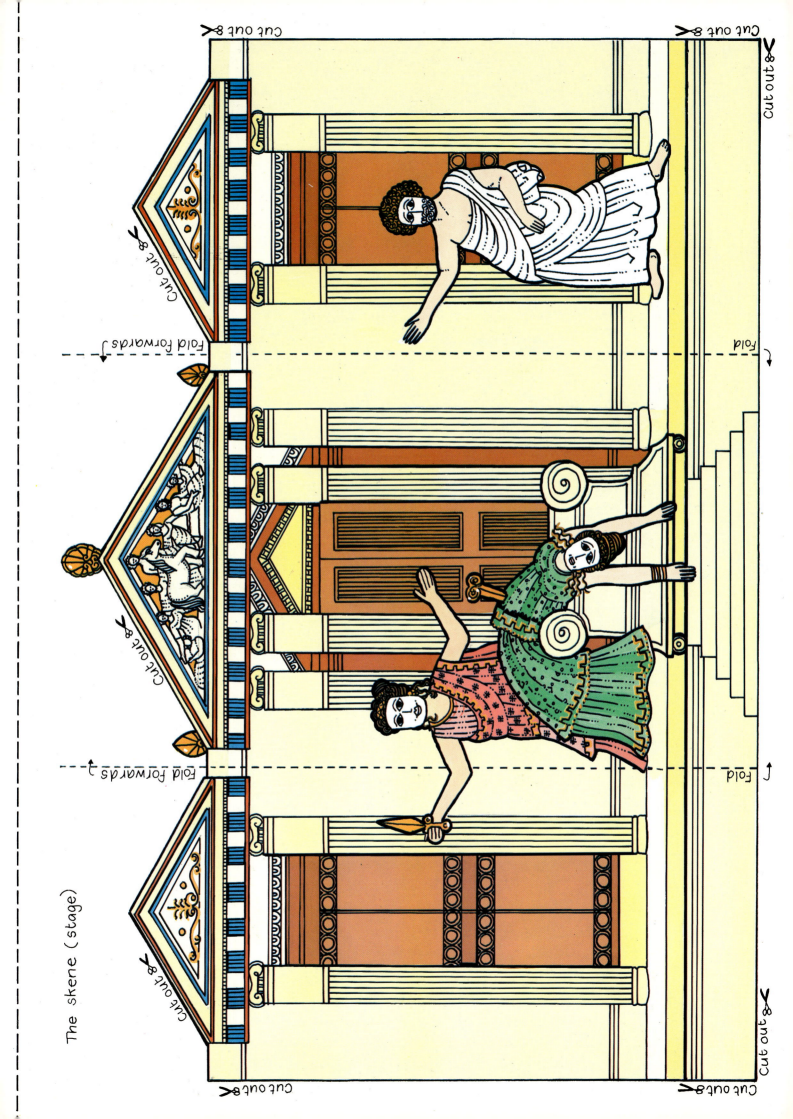

The skene (stage)

Cut out
Cut out
Cut out
Cut out
Cut out
Cut out
Cut out
Cut out
Cut out
Fold Forwards
Fold Forwards
Fold
Fold